FreedomInk presents...

Poetic Meter

&

Random Prose

FreedomInk Publishing

PO Box 161965 Atlanta, GA 30354

Copyright 2013, FreedomInk

All rights reserved. No part of this publication may be reproduced or transmitted in any form or by any means, electronic or mechanical, including photocopy, recording, or any information storage and retrieval system, without permission in writing from the copyright owner.

Cover design by Elaina Lee.

Page layout by FreedomInk Publishing.

Final edit by Katandra Shanel Jackson and Ramona Jones.

ISBN 978-0-98510-416-0

Printed in the United States of America

http://www.freedomink365.com

Also available at FreedomInk

Redemption

Tony's Tiffany

Angel Eyes: A Collective Memoir of Child Sexual Abuse

Life & Love Through My Eyes

The Bride Diaries

Save Me

Loves Me Not Volume 1, Beautiful Broken Me

Loves Me Not Volume 2, The Purge

Loves Me Not, Volume 3, Miracles & Blessings

Coming soon to a bookstore near you!

Dismissed Inhibitions

Woman on Fire

Anybody's Somebody

Good Things To Those Who Wait

Unspoken

Reckoning

A Special Thanks

Thank you to each Author-Poet-Contributor that submitted their works. Thank you for allowing FreedomInk to share your words with the world. Poetry is the tie that binds… We are from this point out and will remain forever more, connected by the invisible, proverbial, literal umbilical cord that sustains the very thing that life is made of. DREAMS! Here's to the beat of each heart, the flick of each wrist, the wit of each alike mind. Even when the poems don't rhyme and the prose is indeed grossly random, we march on to the beat of that silent drum. Poetry is the tie that binds, not just you and I, each author whose work appears in the pages that follow… It binds us all, each to one another. Thank you for providing your own flesh and ~~blood~~ words.

~Katandra Shanel Jackson,

CEO of FreedomInk Publishing

Introduction of Anthology

Seemingly random words joined together for a purpose. That's what it's all about. Words, without aim, finding their rightful place and they tell of the joy and pain of our lives. FreedomInk Presents Poetic Meter & Random Prose is a collection of those words that have found their place. You will read of happiness, sadness, laughter, and pain. The words aren't to make you feel sad. They are to uplift and inspire. They are to transcend our thinking and take us each to a place of peace and triumph. Listen as these Poets express what's on their mind and share what has been inside waiting to be revealed. FreedomInk proudly presents Poetic Meter & Random Prose.

~Ramona 'Jonesy' Jones,

COO of FreedomInk Publishing

Table of Poetry with Contributing Authors

A Special Thanks by Katandra Shanel Jackson, CEO of FreedomInk Publishing   Page 7

Introduction of Anthology by Ramona Jones, COO of FreedomInk Publishing   Page 9

Introducing: Angel Barrueta

Expectations	Page 13
Stars	Page 14
Half Dead	Page 15
Death	Page 16
Ghost/Echo	Page 17
Love	Page 18
My Life	Page 19

Jina & Allen {Mrs. & Mr. Kidd}

Torture	Page 20
House of Mirrors	Page 21

Tamesha 'Danovel' Tolliver

Heart Thrust Upon the Floor	Page 23

Jantzen Alexander

Stranded Thoughts	Page 25
Joy Driven	Page 27
The TRUE Position of Cancer	Page 29

Berlinda White

Still	Page 31
Nothing	Page 33

Katandra Shanel Jackson

Love Is A Luxury	Page 36
When It Rains	Page 37
Silently Observing (My Mother)	Page 39

Ramona Jones

Slipping Away	Page 40
Give It Some Time	Page 41
I Cry	Page 43

Courtney White a.k.a Phoenix

Hello New York	Page 45
It Is Time	Page 49
Defined Definition	Page 51

Timothy Bain

Still I Write	Page 53

Sonya Stegall

Desire To Recite Spoken Words	Page 54

~WRITE~

Insert your title, poem & name here…	Pages 55-58

Fin

Publishing House Profile	Page 59

FreedomInk presents...

Poetic Meter

&

Random Prose

Expectations

Why do they expect me to do everything?
I'm no god
So why do they expect everything
From nothing?
I have no talent
No intelligence
What's with the expectations?
I don't want to do anything
But I need to do something
Expression is the only way that I know that this is real
This life is meaningless but hopeful
I give no hope
Because I know that I need none
What's to hope for?
The world is dying
So why the expectations?
I don't expect anyone to do something or ,even ,
anything
So why do you expect me to do everything?
I am single person
In a universe full of people
Humans are dependent
No one likes to be truly alone
And no one can do anything alone
I need people like me
To help fulfill
Your expectations

~Angel Barrueta

Stars

I miss the stars
They were bright
I loved them
When I was scared
I went outside
And I would lay and look at them
I miss them
I live in the city now
The beautiful pieces of nature that used to surround me
Is long gone
They were replaced by alleys and streets
Ugly, gray buildings
I can barely see the moon now
My heart and soul will always be with the stars
Bright, illuminated objects
In the dark night sky

~Angel Barrueta

Half Dead

I would like to live
A wonderful life
But ,yet, I can't
'Cause I am half-dead
I do not say that I am half-alive
'Cause I have no right to live
I was born a mistake
Brought by mischief
Bringer of new diseases
I live in a place
Where I am alone
Praying for someone to love me
So that I can live my life
And finally say that I am half-alive

~Angel Barrueta

Death

Death is truly the end
It is the end to something beautiful
Life
Those who don't understand life
Think Death is the only way out
But some find another way out
Love and Happiness
They could find someone who makes them happy
Or find someone that they love
And then realize that Death isn't the only way out
It is just an illusion created by the fear and sorrow in your soul
So find a way to make yourself happy
Or find someone that loves you

~Angel Barrueta

Ghost / Echo

I am just a ghost

The voice no one hears

The only time I am heard

Is when I'm too loud to ignore

I am an echo

Repeating what others do

I am a clone

A copy of the original

Destined to live a similar life

Never once being different

So what happens when I break away

Become different

The odd man out?

~Angel Barrueta

Love

Love is something that I don't feel
There's no one to give it to me
My parents disowned me
I have no other family
No friends
Nobody
So why do I feel like I know where to find love?
Why is she smiling at me?
I think I see her
Maybe...
I don't care
I don't feel anything, right?
I feel loved
But why?
There's no one to love me
She talks to me
And for once in my life
I'm sure that I feel love
With her help I'm sure I can feel
Once again
It feels good
Love is like a key
You don't like it
Until you find the lock
And find out who's inside

~Angel Barrueta

My Life

My mind is weird
I am crazy
Life is strange
It's fragile but completely strong at the same time
I get confused at times
About where I should go
Go here, there, maybe everywhere
The world is spinning
Yet I feel calm
The decisions I make
Are good and bad
What do I do when I reach a dead end?
I make a new road
And I let everyone go
I wait and wait for my turn
Once I'm there the road is broken and they all blame me
I can't respond
I don't know what to do
So I sit and shut everyone away
But I don't have too they already have
So I sit in peace and quiet
Until I need to help the others
I get a brilliant idea and I propose it
They shun me while taking my idea
I am forgotten
But then I am needed
I refuse and they beg
Then someone else gets shunned
I help them and we become friends and I am loved
But later I am forgotten
And wait patiently for someone to need and love me
once again

~Angel Barrueta

Torture

I can find no peace, yet am not at war
I fear, I hope I burn, yet I am of ice
I fly above the skies
and am laid low on the ground
I can grasp nothing
yet embrace the whole world
He has put me in a prison which will not open
Yet is not locked
He does not consider me his
But my bonds are not loosened
and love does not cure me or heal me
it will not let me live or free me from this
predicament
I am blind but can see
am mute but can scream
I long to die and ask for help,
and hate myself but love another.
I feed on grief, laugh while I cry
Both life and death vex me;
and yet as I burned
the treacherous world made me worship a beautiful
face.
I say
Never leave me condemned to hell in the eternal life
of your severity

~Jina Kidd

House Of Mirrors

Here I am again, trapped in this place. I can't see my hand in front of my face. The cell is almost as if im trapped by glass. It's not brick, it's too smooth. But I can't break it, alas. How did I get myself in such darkness? Feeling nothing. Almost heartless... A light explodes from the ceiling, Another person in front of me, revealing. And it is clear glass between us. I was right. But strong it won't break. No matter how I fight. He is on the floor, wrapped in chains. Laughing hysterically, like he has no brains. There is no one here for him, other than me. He just lays there laughing, to such an extreme. Another light snaps on, this time to my right. And there lies another individual, crying in the dim light. Again the glass between us stops me from escaping this. I almost got to give props to the man shaping this. Also bound in ropes and chains, from head to toe. Crying, screaming: "Please Let Me GO!" He pleads, begs me to release him, but im too scared. He cries like someone whose last breath he took unprepared. I take a look back at these two, and then another. The emotions are truly from one extreme to the other. A third dim light comes on. This time behind me. Another person laying there. But that didn't surprise me. What did, for starters, is that this man was not bound. Not by ropes, or chains. He was free to move around. But he didn't move. He just lied there, like he didn't care. From what I could tell he was alive. And that he was aware. I called out to him, and all I heard was "Whatever." An apathetic response. Almost like he would lay there forever. A few feet away, another light to show another person. Also unbound. Standing trying to escape. In a rage fearsome. He kicked and screamed like a rabid animal caged. Trying to get free, but to no avail. Making him more enraged.

As I looked at the people around me, I noticed something strange. They were all very similar. Same everything as me without change. Then a man walked in a side door and said to me "The show is starting" I over heard him say to someone else that "This man's mind is departing." Then, a huge curtain opened. Lighting up everything around me. There were people standing everywhere, just looking, pointing toward me. I looked around and saw that I am alone. That brought me the cold shivers. Because I just realized I'm trapped. Never to escape the house of mirrors.

~Allen Kidd

Heart Thrust Upon the Floor

I am being dragged along
My heart thrusting upon the floor
I was spat at and then kissed
And have the nerve to want more
I love you, I hate you
It's the loneliness I abhor
I still want you in my grasp
Even when my heart is thrusting upon the floor.
You taunted me, and then hugged me
Said sweet words then disappeared
Could you be a hallucination?
Am I inflicting my own pain?
Go to sleep crying, Wake up in a cold sweat
And I dare myself not to call your name
But with all the shaking and trembling
I realize this is not a game
That I need you
That I want you
And I will have you again
I finally get up the courage
To have this conversation
I can't stand this life without you
Would you review my resignation?
My Eyes welled up in tears
Continued flashes of my fears
Emptiness in her eyes
With a huge hole in her ear
Seen my words fly out the other
We just ended up undercover
Loneliness for me will forever and always be

Nevermore
But I say this with all confidence
Even, when my heart is still thrusting upon the floor.

~Tamesha 'Danovel' Tolliver

Stranded Thoughts

You were a piece of lint in my hair moons back.

Two birds told me you were no good.
So I released you.

Today, our friendship has proven
to be a bittersweet fact.

Whether or not, trust should be granted
might please you.

I've spoken love in various bodily languages.
I've loved with my eyes, my hands and even my thoughts.

Unfortunately for you, my mind has various passages.

No man truly conceives his actual penetration
into my heart.

I've spoken love in verses on paper,
on the phone, in the air.

I've shouted it from rooftops
and have even left love bare.

I've arrested love and locked it away for permanence.

Every time I do that,
I get coaxed into letting it advance.

I've spoken love through sex,
whether it was rape or desired.

My silence allowed two suspects
to live in the free world.

My love for myself was misplaced
by fear of being revealed.

The good girl I once saw in the mirror
has been killed.

I died seven years ago at the hands
of the Greedy Marquis.

My Cool Breeze was drenched in the blood
flowing beneath me.

He can't accept the full blame for the gruesome night.

My screams should never have been heard.
I should have been out of sight.

When I say I love a man,
I don't mean the depth or weight.

Take my words as rhythmic drums that are never late.

You and I in the same place warrants
that feeling fought.

The actual prospect, however,
is lost in stranded thoughts.

~Jantzen Alexander

Joy-Driven

No longer will I falsely profess my happiness,

The contentment I desire is void of pain and stress.

No more in and out good days and moments.

Today, I seek the joy God specifically for me has woven.

I don't have to pretend to be glad in stormy weather.

My joy isn't affected by happenings. I'm getting it together.

No more borrowed tears from my grandparents.

Today, the spell is broken, and it's all apparent.

No more life granted to a depressed state of mind.

I plan to enjoy the future days my life will find.

I've grown tired of being sad, hopeless and distressed.

I was missing out on my full potential at its best.

Joy is what I desire from God. For in it, I'll find praise.

Today is the day I piece the puzzle of what's supposed to be me.

No longer will I lend the Drunken Defeat the wheel of my car.

I've been in bondage long enough. Twenty-seven years is far too much.

Today, I am re-claiming my self-esteem,

Which is smeared by abandonment, rape and self-hate.

Today, I am appreciating the beauty of being me, and the rich possibilities and opportunities to take.

Today, I emerge from the hoopty of failure

And make a down payment on the Mercedes of Betterment.

False hopes will no longer invade my personal space.

As I keep my eyes on my eternal prize, I will remain optimistic on this joy-drive.

~Jantzen Alexander

The TRUE Position of Cancer

People think of me as a death sentence when they hear the sounding of my name…

Why do you give me so much power? Why allow me to cause you pain? I was created to build your faith, to make you stronger at your weakest point. I may alter your appearance, but NEVER allow me to steal your joy. Use your association with me to build your testimony. Gain strength in knowing I exist. You are more beautiful NOW than ever before. You have to see past yourself to acknowledge it. Can Cancer truly be a beautiful thing? Yes, if you can understand the meaning of my seat. I don't mark the END of your life, but a BRAND NEW beginning. Just because some earthly doctor diagnosed me to you, don't count yourself out of the race. Keep winning!!!! All hope is NOT lost. I have just changed your plans. You can still do what you always dreamed. Enjoy life's dance! Be open about your experience. Educate your daughters and sons. Be strong in the face of my adversity. Don't accept me as your own.

People think of me as a death sentence when they hear the sounding of my name…

Refuse to give me the benefit of your power. Don't allow me to cause you any pain. In God, you ought to plant your seeds of faith. He is the Ultimate Healer, who will NEVER forsake you.

You are stronger NOW than ever before. You just have to see past yourself to acknowledge it…

~Jantzen Alexander

Still

They wanted me to cover it up like I was buried 6 feet deep
They wanted me to conceal the truth like a lost sock mid-week
They wanted me to deny my feelings and pain
They wanted me to run inside get out of the rain
They wanted me to caress the killers, console the moles
They wanted me to give in my badge not play the role
They wanted the mystery not to be my story
They wanted me to die and take this pain to glory
Spill out my shame in my father's name
Yet far away from the lights
Not near any of my rights
Where only angels could hear
Then their coast would be clear
They wanted me to die in shame
Still, walk around here like nobody's to blame
They wanted me to uncross my 't' and not dot my 'I'
They wanted me to hover in the corner and cry
What they asked of me is too much for sure   I might as well
deny being, black, deny I'm a woman and all that
Internally what they say, has nothing to do with me
Still I'm a soul I gotta live like I believe
They didn't know I don't do it for me
I don't just because of humanism challenge equality
I remember my steps
I remember my carved place
Who would I be to submit and lie about my journey

and way
page
Still there is no bitterness in the rain
I use those tears to encourage my way
Bathe any Human shame away
Still I'm not bitter
I love you like yesterday
All brethren though we not blood
Your fear keeps you lying enough
I choose to be free, when I transition
I will be who I was meant to be
Still

~Berlinda White

Nothing

So you joined in on everything, every opportunity in sight
Anything vain to exclaim your name and your game even in a mirror every chance you can
put pictures up saying here I am
Talking bout how hot, how fab, how much swag you had
even anything to make someone else the butt of your laughs
thought you were some type of chief, I will laugh
keep that absurdity please
keeping up with the ignorance
yet mad when somebody calls you a buffoon
I don't need to watch cartoons
you adults give me plenty laughter each afternoon
nothing analytical about you
not even boy scout skills surround you
never could master, the block, rock, the green
never could understand chest if you know what I mean
spend so much time following a stranger
just to hop up and say I hate ya
on social media put everybody on blast
Won't watch the news cause you some dumb lad
as they pass the laws to seal you fate
as they prepare to find a another routine reason
to send a figure upstate,
you too busy, swear you don't have enough time
to pay attention, to the politics of their poisoned minds

yet you can take the time to try and understand
where women of hip hop and they player boyfriends stand
analyzing kindergarten raps
from ex dope selling chaps
yet when it comes to your life you know
nothing about that
when they have stolen from you, even almost your soul
you gonna scream "They so cold!"
as they conquer you in areas where laws have yet to be created
they like how openly you follow what they have created
you say they are monsters, yet they never had to use fear to suck you in
and as the billions of computers analyze your makings
even the drops of your blood have been traced by agents
the greatest trick of an intruder was to make you believe he wasn't
as we look up and realize one day under quarantines, laws and fences
when we look back at all their false pretenses
we will realize our vanity
instead of our compassion
our flagrant absurdity let this action ease in with full traction
even babies will ask how could parents be so dumb
just don't blame anyone when the earth is no more a place to go on
pat yourself on the back and say yes they won

I sat back and gave them my rights
I'm grown yet I've done NOTHING all my life

~Berlinda White

Love Is A Luxury

Love is a luxury at the bottom of the deep blue sea. A grain of sand trapped. Irritation turns to cultivation. This nuisance remains hidden until harvested. Polished and buffed. A most perfect hole drilled, now wedged between two with a unique identity their own. A plethora of these opaque gems complete the string. Displayed in an open case at Tiffany's. That aquamarine, turquoise, teal most inviting. A gift. Wrapped! A most amazing present. 10th year anniversary. If only she had lived to see. Instead he celebrates the ghost of her memory.

~Katandra Shanel Jackson

When It Rains

When it rains…

My mechanical parts threaten to malfunction
And this Ti^{22} heart stalls

When it rains…

Iridium drops crash from overhead
Drawing attention to mercury filled eyes
That overfill at lower lid
Heavy the brim gives

When it rains…

Poisonous tears spill
Leaving in its wake
The burns each acid trail makes
Branding that once lustrous face
Etched engraved encased
Unhumanly beauty replaced

When it rains…

Metal lace that hangs from nickel plated ears Down to here
Its brilliance once trusted
Now oxidized, rusted
A tightly coiled neck
Show signs of slack

The evidence of corrosion
Trickles down a mirage flesh back

When it rains…

Springs unbend
And lend
Caution to the wind
Wiry hair descends upon
Lithe-ium blades, clavicle, sternum, breast plate??
Inner workings of a clock innards mock
The muffled tick tock of a failing titanium heart
Non-indestructible aluminum legs and arms
Magnetized hands
Polarized feet
Stand in a pool of liquid heat

When it rains…

~Katandra Shanel Jackson

Silently Observing (my Mother)

Watching intently, politely from afar
Although I was raised respectfully
I dismiss the sentiment
"It's rude to stare!"
and I (secretly) continue to glare
Then it happens, slowly
The aura of her character appears
The personification of her soul
Every qualm & whim is revealed
and for the very first time
I see the smile that died
The hopes & dreams she left behind
The 'no way out' state of mind
And I want to run up and give her a hug
Wrap my arms around her neck
Exclaim, "I love you thiiiiiiiiiiiiis much!"
But I haven't done that in years
So out of fear of meeting with resistance that fort
she's built, I remain silent
Watching intently, politely from afar
Although I was raised respectfully
I dismiss the sentiment
"It's rude to stare."
And I (openly) continue to glare

~Katandra Shanel Jackson

Slipping Away

Right there
in front of me…
it's mine for the taking
and I hold tight
never letting go…

Easy going
comfortable feelings…
exploring at every given opportunity
and it seems fine
until…
it starts
slipping away…
like wax from a candle…
slow and deliberate,
drying up when it hits
my heart…
my soul…

You're slipping away
from my grasp…
from my view…
I need you back
where I can see you…
hear you…
touch you…
but,
you're slipping away
from me…
And I don't understand
why…

~Ramona Jones

Give It Some Time

Torn and broken
into a million pieces,
your heart has seen it all
and all that's left
is for someone to pick up the pieces…

Picking up is the easy part
putting your heart back together…
that's the hard part
and suddenly,
I am given that task
of making you love again…
feel again…
hope again…
want again…

Following you as you lead,
you take me in and out
of places
that bring joy, laughter, and pain…

Letting you lead
is what you need
to heal…
but,
it's scary
and lonely

and sometimes,
giving up is right there…

Then the bigger picture
flashes in my mind…
so clear…
I want it
and I reach out…

Not yet…
the pieces aren't back together
Not yet…
the task is not complete
Not yet…
the feeling
the hoping
the wanting
not yet…

Just
give it some time…

~Ramona Jones

I Cry

Flowing freely
very easily
they come…

They stay awhile,
camping out
to catch a glimpse
of that moment
where,
I am vulnerable
and open…
to see where it takes me…

I cry
because as much as I want to,
I can't get in…
I cry
because at times,
you seem so far away…
I cry
because I see the way
you look at me
and I know
what your heart is feeling
even though it betrays
sometimes…

Sometimes I cry
because there's that moment
when you let me in…
that moment
when I experience
your love…
that moment

when I experience
your depth…

And the tears
continue to flow freely…
very easily…
they keep coming…
as
I cry…

~Ramona Jones

Hello New York

Hello New York, I'm fresh off the bus
Fully clothed head to toe and I rarely cuss
I'm a reborn breed, a new millennia southern belle
I speak with intelligence if you can't tell
I packed my things and headed here unexpectedly
Even though I've been intimidated ultimately
I'm here now and no turning back
I came to fulfill the dreams that got off track
I'm here now and very much alone
Not used to doing everything on my own
Afraid of everything and fearing the unknown
If silence is a mistake call me accident prone
But I'm here now, not used to the noise
I was taught to be a faithful Christian with poise
I'm soft spoken and hold degrees of education
Seldom to show anger in common communication
Though not oblivious to adaptation
Trials had my license and registration
I'm in the land of mostly single and rudeness
People without tact that bleed prudeness
It's fast paced and time consuming
There are some put together, others need grooming
The place where the scary part is reality
Too many fish in the sea is a recipe for infidelity
Where homosexuality is no longer a fear
Heterosexuals needing to take a closer look in the mirror
Where sex is spontaneous with no real meaning
"I love you" is as overrated as "Needing"
Where people cuss outside of the context
Where they take your all asking where's the rest?
Where women compete for other women's men
Where caring is perceived as weak and.....
Where priorities don't include love but make time for

lust
Superficial mentalities and social lives are a must
Where the dresses cut low and the breasts must sit high
Where heels are tall enough, if you trip, you'll die
Either keep up or you'll get replaced
You'll be an afterthought....simply erased
Where the boring is where the outcasts remain
Where the daring to be different are in fact all the same
I don't really fit in here but I guess I'll pop a cork
Salutations from me......
Hello New York.........

~Courtney 'Phoenix' White

In an interview, Scott-Heron said of the song "That song was about your mind. You have to change your mind before you change the way you live and the way you move...The thing that's going to change people will be something that no one will ever be able to capture on film. It will just be something you see and all of a sudden you realize 'I'm on the wrong page.

It Is Time

Grandma told me the troubles of the world were warned by the Bible

Sins and no regrets, nobody held liable

The Revolution will not be televised when we minimize clinic visits and the number of partners

It Is Time for fewer pregnancies and more trips to the altars

The Revolution will not be televised when the sanctity of marriage is real and not a figment of imagination

Too much what goes around comes around, Karma's infestation

It Is Time to know love and not just infatuation

To know intimacy and not just lust

Grandma knows these things just and unjust

Grandma knows a time when women were called honey lips and Clementine

The fact that women categorize themselves as the B word is a sign

That the Revolution will not be televised when we ensure and we finally realize

And understand what most can't conceptualize

That It Is Time that we become the kings and queens we have blood from

That we value education and act like we have some

It is time that we fulfill Martin's dream

It is time that we take ours, the crop and the cream

Where music isn't the only way out of the hood

Where music is used as an escape for the misunderstood

The Revolution will not be televised when we decide to put a drought on the materialistic industry

There will be time for more chefs, teachers, or chemistry

There will be more doctors, lawyers, and policeman

There will be more preachers, writers, or librarians

We will decrease the amount of no talent rappers trying to live breezy

Those who do work hard make it look too easy

It Is Time we take a larger look at Passion versus Position

To not do the minimum work and expect the commission

Unfortunately It Is also Time that history repeats itself, hoodie's replace whistles

That case is a joke, too many riddles

Hooded Sweatshirts look like they're armed with heavy artillery missiles?

If they are, I'll be sure to run the next time I see one holding tea and some Skittles

Take advantage of life and the secrets to success, he who hesitates is lost

Too busy making your babies you leave lonely and sell drugs at what cost?

The definition of strength is a provider and minimizes unnecessary roughness in their prime

A true man knows who is real and who is wasting their dime

A true hustler creates his own legal path when there is no way out

This new man doesn't mock or need to copy someone else's route

He spends more time living than convicted of crime

He stands before you not above you and directly addresses the issues

He rationalizes and assists the afflicted and misused

The Revolution will not be televised

The Revolution will not be socially disguised

The Revolution cannot be a sitcom
or rerun at this time

My brothers and sisters, this time, the Revolution will be Live.

~Courtney White a.k.a Phoenix

Defined Definition

To not know the unknown puts my
heart in suspension
Our days continue together with no intermission
Somehow you managed to invade my soul being sly
Has anyone ever told you,
you were the definition of fly?
Personifying sweet confection suga, somethin' refined
The mind you share is infinitely defined
This letter is to my darling baby
I don't know if this is forever…but maybe
What fate has to hold is none of our concern
And our past affairs we have long let burn
By now understand
that I am not a figment of imaginary
Feel free to take my hand if it gets to be scary
You are the definition of dream
you were a previous thought
You were the one I prayed for, an unexpected sought
But now my love
for you plays an unforgettable rhythm
I have faith in your protection, super heroism
You are the greatest story, beautifully told
Something worth mentioning when we get old
You are wonderfully crafted suitable for a queen
Intricately mastered, built just for me
Can we…Hold hands and bask in the moonlight?
Share our passion for progression and take flight?
Love…I would rather share a one person cot
Than be distanced apart on somebody's yacht
Please understand me success is a value of importance
But there is no one else
that can harmonize in co-ordinance
You carefully articulate
the appreciation you have for me

I don't know if this is forever, I'm hoping maybe
My spirit was overlooked by man's blind vision
It's like you sat outside of my life hopin' and wishin'
I wondered why you remained anonymous
for so long
Possibly to show me where the failures went wrong
But I promise you, you will want for nothing no more
If I give nothing else it is that I am sure
This letter is to you my darling baby
I don't know if this is forever, but maybe

~Courtney White a.k.a Phoenix

Still I Write

As day turns to night
I, like the watchman,
Stand guard at my post
My weapon of choice,
Right at my fingertips.
Held captive by the burden
Of the enlightenment of my people
I pressed on.
Reminders of old battle scars
Line my domain
Yet my suffering seem in vain
Angered by the tentativeness
Of a people oppressed
I immortalized the thoughts
Rushing through my head
Like rapid waters.
Ailing from the onset of arthritis
Attacking my limbs
I withdraw myself
Into the safety of my intellect
Focusing on that one
The chosen one
Like the others before
That will lead
My people to the promise land.

~Timothy Bain

Desire to Recite Spoken Words

Continue as you are; soon you will be reciting in a Poetry Bar. Not far away, I can see you being in that place, having the opportunity to open your heart and relieve yourself of heartfelt experiences. As you deliver your soul, the intake is greater. There, I will be to experience the journey of your new beginning. Escaping from the world you once knew and going forward into a world of being free, releasing the intense thoughts that have been a burden on your soul. As you continue, you will begin to feel refreshed and eager to give more because a giver is who you are. You're redistributing yourself towards an endless journey, an endless expedition of dispensing the intense vibes that you have carried for so long. You, crying inside because you finally feel free and know deep within that it's finally meant for you to embrace a crowded room with your words of victory, affection, pleasure, and tenderness. You have the power; the people are under your spell, so continue to deliver your words of astuteness.

~Sonya Stegall

The dragon is defeated by the words of your testimony. What's your story? Write…

PUBLISHING HOUSE PROFILE

May 9, 2008 an ingenious idea implanted itself in my psyche. A bookstore in my small hometown would make the perfect community cornerstone! But what would I call it? What did it mean to me? The written word? The liberties of the press? The freedom of expression? The moniker FreedomInk was thus born. The hopes back in 2008 were simple. Secure a location to own and operate my county's 1st bookstore.

As plans etched in sand would have it, the tides of life occurred and my dreams were left stranded, beached. Yes, life did happen. Winter 2009, I uprooted from my small hometown of Manassas Georgia and settled down near Atlanta, in the city of College Park. Everything was all hustle and bustle. Either move or get ran over. I had a very hard time getting a job and when I finally did, I was rather unhappy, although employed in my chosen education/vocation arena. Working as a Pre-K Teacher brought plenty of smiles throughout the length of each day. But you know what they say; there is always someone, somewhere that will take it upon themselves to make your life a living hell. In short and to say the least, I was unenthralled by the center's Director. I can remember it like it was yesterday. The very last staff meeting I attended. Chafe to the core, I was determined to make a way, my own way!

After much soul searching, I decided to hone and craft my passion. I composed my first compilation of poetry Summer 2010. The literary body is brief but it took me every day of 13 weeks to compose. For some the writing comes easy. Words laced together; poetic meter and random prose. I am an emotional writer. Penning each poem in the depth of my hurt and pain, in the midst of my gladdest, proudest, happiest moments; sometimes able to write several poems in one sitting, sometimes taking several days to write one poem. My first published work, 'A Room of Her Own' is available at Amazon via eBook. If you didn't guess, yes, I am a Virginia Woolf fan. Back to the company profile... Little did I know that releasing my first book was going to be so self-soothing. So satisfying. So surreal. At the same time I had finished 'A Room of Her Own', I had gotten engaged, settled more permanent roots in my new city and was feeling pretty good overall about my decision to be a Published Poet.

The adventure that led me to the publishing aspect of the business ensued as follows. I got engaged and began keeping a blog of my 'Bride To Be' day to day life; the ups, the downs, the ins and outs, the preparation, the changing of plans and so forth and so on. I started sharing that blog with friends and family members and they loved it. They couldn't wait to see what happened next along what was thought to be a smooth road but indeed had more dips and dents and potholes than a Detroit side street in the winter after a freezing and salting! Those same friends and family members raved about how they could see the blog as a book. So I started the arduous journey of 'Seek & Seize A Literary Agent'. I knocked and I knocked and I knocked. Some doors went unanswered. Others opened but soon closed. My story was pretty typical of the moment. With all the Bride and Wedding related manuals, magazines and television shows. It's no wonder I didn't receive a very warm reception. After much knocking and several rejections, I decided to take matters into my own hands.

One day, as I was perusing a poetry magazine while at the Hapeville Library, I ran across an advertisement for a self-publishing company, Bookstand Publishing. I contacted the company. Got the information I needed and proceeded to compose my first non-fiction. You see, what those 'No's failed to realize is that although the outline may seem similar, no two stories are ever alike. My book and another's on the same topic will for the most part be as different as the fingerprints on opposing thumbs. And it is. Each 'Diary of A Bride To Be' book is witty, quirky, funny, zany, hilarious, heartfelt. Some pages will make you cheer the Bride on. Other pages you will feel her pain. Some parts of the books will have you in a fit of laughter. Many fans and followers of The Bride Diaries have reported reading the books in a day's time.

After releasing The Diary of A Bride To Be Book 1: A Reason, A Season or A Lifetime, I was approached by an aspiring Author, Richard McKinney. He had heard from a mutual friend about my forthcoming success as an emerging Author. Not only did Mr. McKinney seek my advice, he sought solace, a home for his debut title. I had no idea what I was doing o where to begin. But one thing I did know for certain, I can do anything I put my mind to. So I set out to learn the ropes of the trade. Together he and I worked side by side to release Redemption. That was Fall 2011. I'd like to say the rest is FreedomInk history.

Since then I have adopted several Authors, released their debut titles, and in some cases, their secondary titles and trilogies. Author/Poet of Life & Love Through My Eyes and Dismissed Inhibitions, Ramona Jones, has taken on the role of Chief Operating Officer. Along with this delegation, much has changed in the life of the CEO. Amongst those changes; a change in mind, a change in heart, a change in address, a change in groom....

What is FreedomInk? FreedomInk is a hybrid publishing company. I have studied both traditional and self-publishing models and I've taken the best of both worlds. The Authors are my family. We each do our part, pull our own weight, support one another and pay our dues. Each potential book undergoes some serious scrutiny. I have yet to publish a book that I as a consumer wouldn't be interested in purchasing and reading. To keep my very biased opinion in check, FreedomInk houses a panel of 'secret readers'. Their feedback further allows me to make the best decision. So that is me, um uh er, FreedomInk, in a nutshell. I hope you have enjoyed this formal introduction to the company as well as the Anthology. I can't wait to share the next compilation, the next batch of amazing Authors and Poets, the next literary work of art. The dragon is defeated by the words of your testimony. What's your story? Write...

www.ingramcontent.com/pod-product-compliance
Lightning Source LLC
Chambersburg PA
CBHW020507100426
42813CB00030B/3149/J